God sat on th
for a long long time.
He frowned and He looked
and He looked and He frowned,
for He couldn't seem to find
someone to laugh and talk with,
to sing and play and walk with
and to tell the real good news
He still had on His mind!

He listened to the waters
that were green, and blue and purple,
but they couldn't say a thing
except chuuuurple
chuuuurple chuuuurple

And that isn't saying much,
now is it?

When the First Man Came

Words by Norman C. Habel
Pictures by Jim Roberts

A PURPLE PUZZLE TREE BOOK
COPYRIGHT©1971 CONCORDIA PUBLISHING HOUSE, ST. LOUIS, MISSOURI

MANUFACTURED IN THE UNITED STATES OF AMERICA
ISBN 0-570-06501-1

Concordia Publishing House

A long, long time ago
on a very sunny day,
God sat upon the ground
and looked at all He made.

For a long, long time
He looked and looked.
He looked at the ants,
and He looked at the snails,
and the clumsy kangaroos
with very funny tails,
at the purple fish,
and the old black crows,
and the camels with a hump
and the happy hippopotamus,
who has very muddy feet
that make a funny sound
like phump
shluuuurphump
shluuuurphump

So God put His ear down to the ground.
And He listened to the land,
and He listened to the tree,
but they only make a sound
like EEEEEEEEEEEEEEEEEEE,
when it's very late at night!

And that isn't saying much,
now is it?

So God listened to the animals
and everything He made,
to the swish of the fish
and the tail of the snail
sliding over a bump,
and the happy hippopotamus,
who has very dirty feet
that make a funny sound
like phump
          shluuuurphump
shluuuurphump

But that isn't saying much,
now is it?

God sat on the ground
for a long, long time,
for He hadn't really found
someone to laugh and talk with,
to sing and play and walk with
and tell the real good news
He still had on His mind.

God sat on the ground
and looked and frowned
on a very sunny day.

God sat on the ground
and held in His hand
a lump of dirt and a lump of clay.
And strange to say
the clay was almost red.
So God squashed
and squeeeeezed
and squoooogled it
until He made a head.

God sat on the ground
and held in His hand
another lump of clay.

And strange to say
He used no paste or glue!
But He squashed
and squeeeeezed
and squooooogled it
and made a boy like you
and you and you
and you and you!

Now the boy's name was Adam,
the old, old word for brown or red,
the color of the clay, you see,
that God had used
to make the first red man.
And if you cut your finger,
you'll see,
quite probably,
that you are just as red inside as he.

God took that boy called Adam,
the first red man there was,
and He held him very close.
For He loved him very much.

God opened Adam's mouth
and blew and blew and blew,
until that boy was breathing
just the way we do.
God laughed with him and talked with him,
He sang with him and walked with him,
for He loved him very much.

Now God was King of all the world.
For God was God, you see!
And Adam was the prince He made
to rule that world for Him,
and care for all the animals
like lots and lots of pets.
So Adam gave them all a name:
the frog and the dog
and the ant and the snail
and the clumsy kangaroo
with a very funny tail,
and the purple fish

and the old black crow
and the camel with a hump
and the happy hippopotamus,
who has very dirty feet
that make a funny sound
like phump
        shluuuurphump
    shluuuurphump

But Adam needed someone special
to make him really happy.
He needed someone extra special
to help him do his best.

Adam needed someone
to be a princess at his side
to help him rule the world for God.
For God was King, you see!
And the world was very wide.

Adam fell asleep one day
and he dreamed of someone special.
He dreamed God took one rib away
and made a lovely girl,
bright and fresh and new
like a very pretty butterfly
just out of its cocoon.
And soon,
and soon,
he woke up from his dream.
And the dream was really true!
A girl was there!
A very pretty girl!
A princess just for him.

Adam called his princess Eve,
for she would live with him each day
and play with him from morn till eve.
And she would give him children
to help him rule the world
the way God told them to!

Adam and Eve were happy
and God was happy too.
For He had someone to laugh with
and He had someone to talk with.
He had someone to play with
and He had someone to walk with,
just the way we do.

OTHER TITLES

SET I

WHEN GOD WAS ALL ALONE 56-1200
WHEN THE FIRST MAN CAME 56-1201
IN THE ENCHANTED GARDEN 56-1202
WHEN THE PURPLE WATERS CAME AGAIN 56-1203
IN THE LAND OF THE GREAT WHITE CASTLE 56-1204
WHEN LAUGHING BOY WAS BORN 56-1205
SET I LP RECORD 79-2200
SET I GIFT BOX (6 BOOKS, 1 RECORD) 56-1206

SET II

HOW TRICKY JACOB WAS TRICKED 56-1207
WHEN JACOB BURIED HIS TREASURE 56-1208
WHEN GOD TOLD US HIS NAME 56-1209
IS THAT GOD AT THE DOOR? 56-1210
IN THE MIDDLE OF A WILD CHASE 56-1211
THIS OLD MAN CALLED MOSES 56-1212
SET II LP RECORD 79-2201
SET II GIFT BOX (6 BOOKS, 1 RECORD) 56-1213

SET III

THE TROUBLE WITH TICKLE THE TIGER 56-1218
AT THE BATTLE OF JERICHO! HO! HO! 56-1219
GOD IS NOT A JACK-IN-A-BOX 56-1220
A LITTLE BOY WHO HAD A LITTLE FLING 56-1221
THE KING WHO WAS A CLOWN 56-1222
SING A SONG OF SOLOMON 56-1223
SET III LP RECORD 79-2202
SET III GIFT BOX (6 BOOKS, 1 RECORD) 56-1224

SET IV

ELIJAH AND THE BULL-GOD BAAL 56-1225
LONELY ELIJAH AND THE LITTLE PEOPLE 56-1226
WHEN ISAIAH SAW THE SIZZLING SERAPHIM 56-1227
A VOYAGE TO THE BOTTOM OF THE SEA 56-1228
WHEN JEREMIAH LEARNED A SECRET 56-1229
THE CLUMSY ANGEL AND THE NEW KING 56-1230
SET IV LP RECORD 79-2203
SET IV GIFT BOX (6 BOOKS, 1 RECORD) 56-1231

SET V

THE FIRST TRUE SUPER STAR 56-1242
A WILD YOUNG MAN CALLED JOHN 56-1243
THE DIRTY DEVIL AND THE CARPENTERS BOY 56-1244
WHEN JESUS DID HIS MIRACLES OF LOVE 56-1245
WHEN JESUS TOLD HIS PARABLES 56-1246
OLD ROCK THE FISHERMAN 56-1247
SET V LP RECORD 79-2204
SET V GIFT BOX 56-1248

SET VI

WONDER BREAD FROM A BOY'S LUNCH 56-1249
WHEN JESUS RODE IN THE PURPLE PUZZLE
   PARADE 56-1250
   WHEN JESUS' FRIENDS BETRAYED HIM 56-1251
   THE DEEP DARK DAY WHEN JESUS DIED 56-1252
   DANCE, LITTLE ALLELU, WITH ME 56-1253
   THE KEY TO THE PURPLE PUZZLE TREE 56-1254
   SET VI LP RECORD 79-2205
   SET VI GIFT BOX 56-1255

the PURPLE PUZZLE TREE